M

Happy Days

WORKS BY SAMUEL BECKETT PUBLISHED BY GROVE PRESS

Collected Poems in English and French

The Collected Shorter Plays
(All That Fall, Act Without Words I,
Act Without Words II, Krapp's Last Tape,
Rough for Theatre I, Rough for Theatre II,
Embers, Rough for Radio I, Rough for
Radio II, Words and Music, Cascando,
Play, Film, The Old Tune, Come and Go,
Eh Joe, Breath, Not I, That Time, Footfalls,
Ghost Trio, . . . but the clouds . . . , A Piece
of Monologue, Rockaby, Ohio Impromptu,
Quad, Catastrophe, Nacht and Träume,
What Where)

The Complete Short Prose: 1929–1989
(Assumption, Sedendo et Quiescendo,
Text, A Case in a Thousand, First Love, The
Expelled, The Calmative, The End, Texts for
Nothing 1–13, From an Abandoned Work,
The Image, All Strange Away, Imagination
Dead Imagine, Enough, Ping, Lessness,
The Lost Ones, Fizzles 1–8, Heard in the
Dark 1, Heard in the Dark 2, One Evening,
As the story was told, The Cliff, neither,
Stirrings Still, Variations on a "Still" Point,
Faux Départs, The Capital of the Ruins)

Disjecta: Miscellaneous Writings and
a Dramatic Fragment

Endgame and Act Without Words

Ends and Odds

First Love and Other Shorts

Happy Days

How It Is

I Can't Go On, I'll Go On:
A Samuel Beckett Reader

Krapp's Last Tape
(All That Fall, Embers, Act Without Words I,
Act Without Words II)

Mercier and Camier

Molloy

More Pricks Than Kicks
(Dante and the Lobster, Fingal, Ding-Dong,
A Wet Night, Love and Lethe, Walking Out,
What a Misfortune, The Smeraldina's Billet
Doux, Yellow, Draff)

Murphy

Nohow On
(Company, Ill Seen Ill Said, Worstward Ho)

The Poems, Short Fiction, and Criticism of
Samuel Beckett

Rockaby and Other Short Plays
(Rockaby, Ohio Impromptu, All Strange
Away, and A Piece of Monologue)

The Selected Works of Samuel Beckett
(boxed paperback set)
Volume I: Novels
(Murphy, Watt, Mercier and Camier)
Volume II: Novels
(Molloy, Malone Dies, The Unnamable,
How It Is)
Volume III: Dramatic Works
Volume IV: Poems, Short Fiction, Criticism

Stories and Texts for Nothing
(The Expelled, The Calmative, The End,
Texts for Nothing 1–13)

Three Novels
(Molloy, Malone Dies, The Unnamable)

Waiting for Godot

Waiting for Godot: A Bilingual Edition

Watt

Samuel Beckett

Happy Days

Grove Press
New York

Happy Days

The world premiere of *Happy Days* was presented by Theatre 1962 (Messrs. Richard Barr and Clinton Wilder) at the Cherry Lane Theatre, New York, on September 17, 1961, directed by Alan Schneider and designed by William Ritman, with the following cast:

WINNIE   Ruth White

WILLIE   John C. Becher

Winnie, *a woman about fifty*
Willie, *a man about sixty*

ACT I

Expanse of scorched grass rising centre to low mound. Gentle slopes down to front and either side of stage. Back an abrupter fall to stage level. Maximum of simplicity and symmetry.

Blazing light.

Very pompier trompe-l'oeil backcloth to represent unbroken plain and sky receding to meet in far distance.

Imbedded up to above her waist in exact centre of mound, Winnie. About fifty, well preserved, blond for preference, plump, arms and shoulders bare, low bodice, big bosom, pearl necklet. She is discovered sleeping, her arms on the ground before her, her head on her arms. Beside her on ground to her left a capacious black bag, shopping

variety, and to her right a collapsible collapsed parasol, beak of handle
emerging from sheath.

To her right and rear, lying asleep on ground, hidden by mound,
Willie.

Long pause. A bell rings piercingly, say ten seconds, stops.
She does not move. Pause. Bell more piercingly, say five seconds.
She wakes. Bell stops. She raises her head, gazes front. Long pause.
She straightens up, lays her hands flat on ground, throws back her
head and gazes at zenith. Long pause.

WINNIE [*gazing at zenith*] Another heavenly day. [*Pause. Head back level, eyes front, pause. She clasps hands to breast, closes eyes. Lips move in inaudible prayer, say ten seconds. Lips still. Hands remain clasped. Low.*] For Jesus Christ sake Amen. [*Eyes open, hands unclasp, return to mound. Pause. She clasps hands to breast again, closes eyes, lips move again in inaudible addendum, say five seconds. Low.*] World without end Amen. [*Eyes open, hands unclasp, return to mound. Pause.*] Begin, Winnie. [*Pause.*] Begin your day, Winnie. [*Pause. She turns to bag, rummages in it without moving it from its place, brings out toothbrush,

*rummages again, brings out flat tube of toothpaste, turns
back front, unscrews cap of tube, lays cap on ground,
squeezes with difficulty small blob of paste on brush, holds
tube in one hand and brushes teeth with other. She turns
modestly aside and back to her right to spit out behind
mound. In this position her eyes rest on Willie. She spits out.
She cranes a little further back and down. Loud.]* Hoo-oo!
[Pause. Louder.] Hoo-oo! *[Pause. Tender smile as she turns
back front, lays down brush.]* Poor Willie—*[examines tube,
smile off]*—running out—*[looks for cap]*—ah well—
[finds cap]—can't be helped—*[screws on cap]*—just one
of those old things—*[lays down tube]*—another of
those old things—*[turns towards bag]*—just can't be
cured—*[rummages in bag]*—cannot be cured—*[brings
out small mirror, turns back front]*—ah yes—*[inspects
teeth in mirror]*—poor dear Willie—*[testing upper front
teeth with thumb, indistinctly]*—good Lord!—*[pulling
back upper lip to inspect gums, do]*—good God!—*[pulling
back corner of mouth, mouth open, do]*—ah well—*[other
corner, do]*—no worse—*[abandons inspection, normal
speech]*—no better, no worse—*[lays down mirror]*—no
change—*[wipes fingers on grass]*—no pain—*[looks for
toothbrush]*—hardly any—*[takes up toothbrush]*—great

thing that—[*examines handle of brush*]—nothing like
it—[*examines handle, reads*]—pure . . . what?—
[*pause*]—what?—[*lays down brush*]—ah yes—[*turns
towards bag*]—poor Willie—[*rummages in bag*]—no
zest—[*rummages*]—for anything—[*brings out spectacles
in case*]—no interest—[*turns back front*]—in life—
[*takes spectacles from case*]—poor dear Willie—[*lays
down case*]—sleep for ever—[*opens spectacles*]—
marvellous gift—[*puts on spectacles*]—nothing to touch
it—[*looks for toothbrush*]—in my opinion—[*takes up
toothbrush*]—always said so—[*examines handle of
brush*]—wish I had it—[*examines handle, reads*]—
genuine . . . pure . . . what?—[*lays down brush*]—blind
next—[*takes off spectacles*]—ah well—[*lays down
spectacles*]—seen enough—[*feels in bodice for
handkerchief*]—I suppose—[*takes out folded
handkerchief*]—by now—[*shakes out handkerchief*]—
what are those wonderful lines—[*wipes one eye*]—woe
woe is me—[*wipes the other*]—to see what I see—[*looks
for spectacles*]—ah yes—[*takes up spectacles*]—wouldn't
miss it—[*starts polishing spectacles, breathing on lenses*]—
or would I?—[*polishes*]—holy light—[*polishes*]—bob
up out of dark—[*polishes*]—blaze of hellish light.

[*Stops polishing, raises face to sky, pause, head back level, resumes polishing, stops polishing, cranes back to her right and down.*] Hoo-oo! [*Pause. Tender smile as she turns back front and resumes polishing. Smile off.*] Marvellous gift—[*stops polishing, lays down spectacles*]—wish I had it—[*folds handkerchief*]—ah well—[*puts handkerchief back in bodice*]—can't complain—[*looks for spectacles*]—no no—[*takes up spectacles*]—mustn't complain—[*holds up spectacles, looks through lens*]—so much to be thankful for—[*looks through other lens*]—no pain—[*puts on spectacles*]—hardly any—[*looks for toothbrush*]—wonderful thing that—[*takes up toothbrush*]—nothing like it—[*examines handle of brush*]—slight headache sometimes—[*examines handle, reads*]—guaranteed . . . genuine . . . pure . . . what?—[*looks closer*]—genuine pure . . . —[*takes handkerchief from bodice*]—ah yes—[*shakes out handkerchief*]—occasional mild migraine—[*starts wiping handle of brush*]—it comes—[*wipes*]—then goes—[*wiping mechanically*]—ah yes—[*wiping*]—many mercies—[*wiping*]—great mercies—[*stops wiping, fixed lost gaze, brokenly*]—prayers perhaps not for naught—[*pause, do*]—first thing—[*pause, do*]—last thing—[*head down, resumes wiping, stops wiping, head up, calmed, wipes eyes, folds handkerchief, puts it back in bodice, examines handle of brush, reads]*—fully guaranteed . . . genuine pure . . . —*[looks closer]*— genuine pure . . . *[Takes off spectacles, lays them and brush down, gazes before her.]* Old things. *[Pause.]* Old eyes. *[Long pause.]* On, Winnie. *[She casts about her, sees parasol, considers it at length, takes it up and develops from sheath a handle of surprising length. Holding butt of parasol in right hand she cranes back and down to her right to hang over Willie.]* Hoo-oo! *[Pause.]* Willie! *[Pause.]* Wonderful gift. *[She strikes down at him with beak of parasol.]* Wish I had it. *[She strikes again. The parasol slips from her grasp and falls behind mound. It is immediately restored to her by Willie's invisible hand.]* Thank you, dear. *[She transfers parasol to left hand, turns back front and examines right palm.]* Damp. *[Returns parasol to right hand, examines left palm.]* Ah well, no worse. *[Head up, cheerfully.]* No better, no worse, no change. *[Pause. Do.]* No pain. *[Cranes back to look down at Willie, holding parasol by butt as before.]* Don't go off on me again now dear will you please, I may need you. *[Pause.]* No hurry, no hurry, just don't curl up on me again. *[Turns back front, lays down parasol, examines palms together, wipes*

them on grass.] Perhaps a shade off colour just the
same. [*Turns to bag, rummages in it, brings out revolver,
holds it up, kisses it rapidly, puts it back, rummages, brings
out almost empty bottle of red medicine, turns back front,
looks for spectacles, puts them on, reads label.*] Loss of
spirits . . . lack of keenness . . . want of appetite . . .
infants . . . children . . . adults . . . six level . . .
tablespoonfuls daily—[*head up, smile*]—the old
style!—[*smile off, head down, reads*]—daily . . . before
and after . . . meals . . . instantaneous . . . [*looks
closer*] . . . improvement. [*Takes off spectacles, lays them
down, holds up bottle at arm's length to see level, unscrews
cap, swigs it off head well back, tosses cap and bottle away
in Willie's direction. Sound of breaking glass.*] Ah that's
better! [*Turns to bag, rummages in it, brings out lipstick,
turns back front, examines lipstick.*] Running out.
[*Looks for spectacles.*] Ah well. [*Puts on spectacles, looks for
mirror.*] Musn't complain. [*Takes up mirror, starts doing
lips.*] What is that wonderful line? [*Lips.*] Oh fleeting
joys—[*lips*]—oh something lasting woe. [*Lips. She is
interrupted by disturbance from Willie. He is sitting up.
She lowers lipstick and mirror and cranes back and down to
look at him. Pause. Top back of Willie's bald head, trickling*

blood, rises to view above slope, comes to rest. Winnie pushes up her spectacles. Pause. His hand appears with handkerchief, spreads it on skull, disappears. Pause. The hand appears with boater, club ribbon, settles it on head, rakish angle, disappears. Pause. Winnie cranes a little further back and down.] Slip on your drawers, dear, before you get singed. [*Pause.*] No? [*Pause.*] Oh I see, you still have some of that stuff left. [*Pause.*] Work it well in, dear. [*Pause.*] Now the other. [*Pause. She turns back front, gazes before her. Happy expression.*] Oh this is going to be another happy day! [*Pause. Happy expression off. She pulls down spectacles and resumes lips. Willie opens newspaper, hands invisible. Tops of yellow sheets appear on either side of his head. Winnie finishes lips, inspects them in mirror held a little further away.*] Ensign crimson. [*Willie turns page. Winnie lays down lipstick and mirror, turns towards bag.*] Pale flag. [*Willie turns page. Winnie rummages in bag, brings out small ornate brimless hat with crumpled feather, turns back front, straightens hat, smooths feather, raises it towards head, arrests gesture as Willie reads.*]

WILLIE His Grace and Most Reverend Father in God Dr. Carolus Hunter dead in tub.

[*Pause.*]

WINNIE [*gazing front, hat in hand, tone of fervent reminiscence*]
Charlie Hunter! [*Pause.*] I close my eyes—[*she takes off
spectacles and does so, hat in one hand, spectacles in other,
Willie turns page*]—and am sitting on his knees again,
in the back garden at Borough Green, under the
horse-beech. [*Pause. She opens eyes, puts on spectacles,
fiddles with hat.*] Oh the happy memories!

[*Pause. She raises hat towards head, arrests gesture as
Willie reads.*]

WILLIE Opening for smart youth.

[*Pause. She raises hat towards head, arrests gesture, takes
off spectacles, gazes front, hat in one hand, spectacles
in other.*]

WINNIE My first ball! [*Long pause.*] My second ball! [*Long pause.
Closes eyes.*] My first kiss! [*Pause. Willie turns page.
Winnie opens eyes.*] A Mr. Johnson, or Johnston, or
perhaps I should say Johnstone. Very bushy

moustache, very tawny. [*Reverently.*] Almost ginger!
[*Pause.*] Within a toolshed, though whose I cannot
conceive. We had no toolshed and he most certainly
had no toolshed. [*Closes eyes.*] I see the piles of pots.
[*Pause.*] The tangles of bast. [*Pause.*] The shadows
deepening among the rafters.

[*Pause. She opens eyes, puts on spectacles, raises hat towards
head, arrests gesture as Willie reads.*]

WILLIE Wanted bright boy.

[*Pause. Winnie puts on hat hurriedly, looks for mirror.
Willie turns page. Winnie takes up mirror, inspects hat, lays
down mirror, turns towards bag. Paper disappears. Winnie
rummages in bag, brings out magnifying-glass, turns back
front, looks for toothbrush. Paper reappears, folded, and
begins to fan Willie's face, hand invisible. Winnie takes up
toothbrush and examines handle through glass.*]

WINNIE Fully guaranteed . . . [*Willie stops fanning*] . . . genuine
pure . . . [*Pause. Willie resumes fanning. Winnie looks
closer, reads.*] Fully guaranteed . . . [*Willie stops*

fanning] . . . genuine pure . . . [*Pause. Willie resumes
fanning. Winnie lays down glass and brush, takes
handkerchief from bodice, takes off and polishes spectacles,
puts on spectacles, looks for glass, takes up and polishes
glass, lays down glass, looks for brush, takes up brush and
wipes handle, lays down brush, puts handkerchief back in
bodice, looks for glass, takes up glass, looks for brush, takes
up brush and examines handle through glass.*] Fully
guaranteed . . . [*Willie stops fanning*] . . . genuine
pure . . . [*pause, Willie resumes fanning*] . . . hog's
[*Willie stops fanning, pause*] . . . setae. [*Pause. Winnie lays
down glass and brush, paper disappears, Winnie takes off
spectacles, lays them down, gazes front.*] Hog's setae.
[*Pause.*] That is what I find so wonderful, that not a day
goes by—[*smile*]—to speak in the old style—[*smile
off*]—hardly a day, without some addition to one's
knowledge however trifling, the addition I mean,
provided one takes the pains. [*Willie's hand reappears
with a postcard which he examines close to eyes.*] And if for
some strange reason no further pains are possible,
why then just close the eyes—[*she does so*]—and wait
for the day to come—[*opens eyes*]—the happy day to
come when flesh melts at so many degrees and the

night of the moon has so many hundred hours. [*Pause.*] That is what I find so comforting when I lose heart and envy the brute beast. [*Turning towards Willie.*] I hope you are taking in— [*She sees postcard, bends lower.*] What is that you have there, Willie, may I see? [*She reaches down with hand and Willie hands her card. The hairy forearm appears above slope, raised in gesture of giving, the hand open to take back, and remains in this position till card is returned. Winnie turns back front and examines card.*] Heavens what are they up to! [*She looks for spectacles, puts them on and examines card.*] No but this is just genuine pure filth! [*Examines card.*] Make any nice-minded person want to vomit! [*Impatience of Willie's fingers. She looks for glass, takes it up and examines card through glass. Long pause.*] What does that creature in the background think he's doing? [*Looks closer.*] Oh no really! [*Impatience of fingers. Last long look. She lays down glass, takes edge of card between right forefinger and thumb, averts head, takes nose between left forefinger and thumb.*] Pah! [*Drops card.*] Take it away! [*Willie's arm disappears. His hand reappears immediately, holding card. Winnie takes off spectacles, lays them down, gazes before her. During what follows Willie continues to relish card,*

varying angles and distance from his eyes.] Hog's setae.
[*Puzzled expression.*] What exactly is a hog? [*Pause. Do.*]
A sow of course I know, but a hog . . . [*Puzzled
expression off.*] Oh well what does it matter, that is what
I always say, it will come back, that is what I find so
wonderful, all comes back. [*Pause.*] All? [*Pause.*] No, not
all. [*Smile.*] No no. [*Smile off.*] Not quite. [*Pause.*] A part.
[*Pause.*] Floats up, one fine day, out of the blue. [*Pause.*]
That is what I find so wonderful. [*Pause. She turns
towards bag. Hand and card disappear. She makes to
rummage in bag, arrests gesture.*] No. [*She turns back front.
Smile.*] No no. [*Smile off.*] Gently Winnie. [*She gazes
front. Willie's hand reappears, takes off hat, disappears with
hat.*] What then? [*Hand reappears, takes handkerchief from
skull, disappears with handkerchief. Sharply, as to one not
paying attention.*] Winnie! [*Willie bows head out of sight.*]
What *is* the alternative? [*Pause.*] What *is* the al— [*Willie
blows nose loud and long, head and hands invisible. She
turns to look at him. Pause. Head reappears. Pause. Hand
reappears with handkerchief, spreads it on skull, disappears.
Pause. Hand reappears with boater, settles it on head, rakish
angle, disappears. Pause.*] Would I had let you sleep on.
[*She turns back front. Intermittent plucking at grass, head

up and down, to animate following.] Ah yes, if only I
could bear to be alone, I mean prattle away with not a
soul to hear. [*Pause.*] Not that I flatter myself you hear
much, no Willie, God forbid. [*Pause.*] Days perhaps
when you hear nothing. [*Pause.*] But days too when
you answer. [*Pause.*] So that I may say at all times, even
when you do not answer and perhaps hear nothing,
Something of this is being heard, I am not merely
talking to myself, that is in the wilderness, a thing I
could never bear to do—for any length of time.
[*Pause.*] That is what enables me to go on, go on
talking that is. [*Pause.*] Whereas if you were to die—
[*smile*]—to speak in the old style—[*smile off*]—or go
away and leave me, then what would I do, what *could* I
do, all day long, I mean between the bell for waking
and the bell for sleep? [*Pause.*] Simply gaze before me
with compressed lips. [*Long pause while she does so. No
more plucking.*] Not another word as long as I drew
breath, nothing to break the silence of this place.
[*Pause.*] Save possibly, now and then, every now and
then, a sigh into my looking-glass. [*Pause.*] Or a
brief . . . gale of laughter, should I happen to see the
old joke again. [*Pause. Smile appears, broadens and seems*

about to culminate in laugh when suddenly replaced by expression of anxiety.] My hair! [*Pause.*] Did I brush and comb my hair? [*Pause.*] I may have done. [*Pause.*] Normally I do. [*Pause.*] There is so little one *can* do. [*Pause.*] One does it all. [*Pause.*] All one can. [*Pause.*] Tis only human. [*Pause.*] Human nature. [*She begins to inspect mound, looks up.*] Human weakness. [*She resumes inspection of mound, looks up.*] Natural weakness. [*She resumes inspection of mound.*] I see no comb. [*Inspects.*] Nor any hairbrush. [*Looks up. Puzzled expression. She turns to bag, rummages in it.*] The comb is here. [*Back front. Puzzled expression. Back to bag. Rummages.*] The brush is here. [*Back front. Puzzled expression.*] Perhaps I put them back, after use. [*Pause. Do.*] But normally I do not put things back, after use, no, I leave them lying about and put them back all together, at the end of the day. [*Smile.*] To speak in the old style. [*Pause.*] The sweet old style. [*Smile off.*] And yet . . . I seem . . . to remember . . . [*Suddenly careless.*] Oh well, what does it matter, that is what I always say, I shall simply brush and comb them later on, purely and simply, I have the whole— [*Pause. Puzzled.*] Them? [*Pause.*] Or it? [*Pause.*] *Brush and comb it?* [*Pause.*] Sounds improper somehow.

[*Pause. Turning a little towards Willie.*] What would you say, Willie? [*Pause. Turning a little further.*] What would you say, Willie, speaking of your hair, them or it? [*Pause.*] The hair on your head, I mean. [*Pause. Turning a little further.*] The hair on your head, Willie, what would you say speaking of the hair on your head, them or it?

[*Long pause.*]

WILLIE It.

WINNIE [*turning back front, joyful*] Oh you are going to talk to me today, this is going to be a happy day! [*Pause. Joy off.*] Another happy day. [*Pause.*] Ah well, where was I, my hair, yes, later on, I shall be thankful for it later on. [*Pause.*] I have my—[*raises hands to hat*]—yes, on, my hat on—[*lowers hands*]—I cannot take it off now. [*Pause.*] To think there are times one cannot take off one's hat, not if one's life were at stake. Times one cannot put it on, times one cannot take it off. [*Pause.*] How often I have said, Put on your hat now, Winnie, there is nothing else for it, take off your hat now,

Winnie, like a good girl, it will do you good, and did not. [*Pause.*] Could not. [*Pause. She raises hand, frees a strand of hair from under hat, draws it towards eye, squints at it, lets it go, hand down.*] Golden you called it, that day, when the last guest was gone—[*hand up in gesture of raising a glass*]—to your golden . . . may it never . . . [*voice breaks*] . . . may it never . . . [*Hand down. Head down. Pause. Low.*] That day. [*Pause. Do.*] What day? [*Pause. Head up. Normal voice.*] What now? [*Pause.*] Words fail, there are times when even they fail. [*Turning a little towards Willie.*] Is that not so, Willie? [*Pause. Turning a little further.*] Is not that so, Willie, that even words fail, at times? [*Pause. Back front.*] What is one to do then, until they come again? Brush and comb the hair, if it has not been done, or if there is some doubt, trim the nails if they are in need of trimming, these things tide one over. [*Pause.*] That is what I mean. [*Pause.*] That is all I mean. [*Pause.*] That is what I find so wonderful, that not a day goes by— [*smile*]—to speak in the old style—[*smile off*]— without some blessing—[*Willie collapses behind slope, his head disappears, Winnie turns towards event*]—in disguise. [*She cranes back and down.*] Go back into your

hole now, Willie, you've exposed yourself enough.
[*Pause.*] Do as I say, Willie, don't lie sprawling there in
this hellish sun, go back into your hole. [*Pause.*] Go on
now, Willie. [*Willie invisible starts crawling left towards
hole.*] That's the man. [*She follows his progress with her
eyes.*] Not head first, stupid, how are you going to
turn? [*Pause.*] That's it . . . right round . . . now . . . back
in. [*Pause.*] Oh I know it is not easy, dear, crawling
backwards, but it is rewarding in the end. [*Pause.*] You
have left your vaseline behind. [*She watches as he crawls
back for vaseline.*] The lid! [*She watches as he crawls back
towards hole. Irritated.*] Not head first, I tell you! [*Pause.*]
More to the right. [*Pause.*] The *right*, I said. [*Pause.
Irritated.*] Keep your tail down, can't you! [*Pause.*] Now.
[*Pause.*] There! [*All these directions loud. Now in her
normal voice, still turned towards him.*] Can you hear me?
[*Pause.*] I beseech you, Willie, just yes or no, can you
hear me, just yes or nothing.

[*Pause.*]

WILLIE   Yes.

WINNIE   [*turning front, same voice*] And now?

WILLIE   [*irritated*] Yes.

WINNIE   [*less loud*] And now?

WILLIE   [*more irritated*] Yes.

WINNIE   [*still less loud*] And now? [*A little louder.*] And now?

WILLIE   [*violently*] Yes!

WINNIE   [*same voice*] Fear no more the heat o' the sun. [*Pause.*]
         Did you hear that?

WILLIE   [*irritated*] Yes.

WINNIE   [*same voice*] What? [*Pause.*] What?

WILLIE   [*more irritated*] Fear no more.
         [*Pause.*]

WINNIE   [*same voice*] No more what? [*Pause.*] Fear no more what?

WILLIE [*violently*] Fear no more!

WINNIE [*normal voice, gabbled*] Bless you Willie I do appreciate
your goodness I know what an effort it costs you, now
you may relax I shall not trouble you again unless I
am obliged to, by that I mean unless I come to the
end of my own resources which is most unlikely, just
to know that in theory you can hear me even though
in fact you don't is all I need, just to feel you there
within earshot and conceivably on the qui vive is all I
ask, not to say anything I would not wish you to hear
or liable to cause you pain, not to be just babbling
away on trust as it is were not knowing and
something gnawing at me. [*Pause for breath.*] Doubt.
[*Places index and second finger on heart area, moves them
about, brings them to rest.*] Here. [*Moves them slightly.*]
Abouts. [*Hand away.*] Oh no doubt the time will come
when before I can utter a word I must make sure you
heard the one that went before and then no doubt
another come another time when I must learn to talk
to myself a thing I could never bear to do such
wilderness. [*Pause.*] Or gaze before me with
compressed lips. [*She does so.*] All day long. [*Gaze and*

lips again.] No. [*Smile.*] No no. [*Smile off.*] There is of
course the bag. [*Turns towards it.*] There will always be
the bag. [*Back front.*] Yes, I suppose so. [*Pause.*] Even
when you are gone, Willie. [*She turns a little towards
him.*] You *are* going, Willie, aren't you? [*Pause. Louder.*]
You *will* be going soon, Willie, won't you? [*Pause.
Louder.*] Willie! [*Pause. She cranes back and down to look
at him.*] So you have taken off your straw, that is wise.
[*Pause.*] You do look snug, I must say, with your chin
on your hands and the old blue eyes like saucers in
the shadows. [*Pause.*] Can you see me from there I
wonder, I still wonder. [*Pause.*] No? [*Back front.*] Oh I
know it does not follow when two are gathered
together—[*faltering*]—in this way—[*normal*]—that
because one sees the other the other sees the one, life
has taught me that . . . too. [*Pause.*] Yes, life I suppose,
there is no other word. [*She turns a little towards him.*]
Could you see me, Willie, do you think, from where
you are, if you were to raise your eyes in my direction?
[*Turns a little further.*] Lift up your eyes to me, Willie,
and tell me can you see me, do that for me, I'll lean
back as far as I can. [*Does so. Pause.*] No? [*Pause.*] Well
never mind. [*Turns back painfully front.*] The earth is

very tight today, can it be I have put on flesh, I trust
not. [*Pause. Absently, eyes lowered.*] The great heat
possibly. [*Starts to pat and stroke ground.*] All things
expanding, some more than others. [*Pause. Patting and
stroking.*] Some less. [*Pause. Do.*] Oh I can well imagine
what is passing through your mind, it is not enough
to have to listen to the woman, now I must look at her
as well. [*Pause. Do.*] Well it is very understandable.
[*Pause. Do.*] Most understandable. [*Pause. Do.*] One
does not appear to be asking a great deal, indeed at
times it would seem hardly possible—[*voice breaks,
falls to a murmur*]—to ask less—of a fellow-creature—
to put it mildly—whereas actually—when you think
about it—look into your heart—see the other—what
he needs—peace—to be left in peace—then perhaps
the moon—all this time—asking for the moon.
[*Pause. Stroking hand suddenly still. Lively.*] Oh I say, what
have we here? [*Bending head to ground, incredulous.*]
Looks like life of some kind! [*Looks for spectacles, puts
them on, bends closer. Pause.*] An emmet! [*Recoils. Shrill.*]
Willie, an emmet, a live emmet! [*Seizes magnifying-
glass, bends to ground again, inspects through glass.*]
Where's it gone? [*Inspects.*] Ah! [*Follows its progress

through grass.] Has like a little white ball in its arms.
[*Follows progress. Hand still. Pause.*] It's gone in.
[*Continues a moment to gaze at spot through glass, then
slowly straightens up, lays down glass, takes off spectacles
and gazes before her, spectacles in hand. Finally.*] Like a
little white ball.

[*Long pause. Gesture to lay down spectacles.*]

WILLIE   Eggs.

WINNIE   [*arresting gesture*] What?

[*Pause.*]

WILLIE   Eggs. [*Pause. Gesture to lay down glasses.*] Formication.

WINNIE   [*arresting gesture*] What?

[*Pause.*]

WILLIE   Formication.

[Pause. She lays down spectacles, gazes before her. Finally.]

WINNIE *[murmur]* God. *[Pause. Willie laughs quietly. After a moment she joins in. They laugh quietly together. Willie stops. She laughs on a moment alone. Willie joins in. They laugh together. She stops. Willie laughs on a moment alone. He stops. Pause. Normal voice.]* Ah well what a joy in any case to hear you laugh again, Willie, I was convinced I never would, you never would. *[Pause.]* I suppose some people might think us a trifle irreverent, but I doubt it. *[Pause.]* How can one better magnify the Almighty than by sniggering with him at his little jokes, particularly the poorer ones? *[Pause.]* I think you would back me up there, Willie. *[Pause.]* Or were we perhaps diverted by two quite different things? *[Pause.]* Oh well, what does it matter, that is what I always say, so long as one . . . you know . . . what is that wonderful line . . . laughing wild . . . something something laughing wild amid severest woe. *[Pause.]* And now? *[Long pause.]* Was I lovable once, Willie? *[Pause.]* Was I ever lovable? *[Pause.]* Do not misunderstand my question, I am not asking you if you loved me, we know all about that, I am asking you

if you found me lovable—at one stage. [*Pause.*] No?
[*Pause.*] You can't? [*Pause.*] Well I admit it is a teaser.
And you have done more than your bit already, for the
time being, just lie back now and relax, I shall not
trouble you again unless I am compelled to, just to
know you are there within hearing and conceivably on
the semi-alert is . . . er . . . paradise enow. [*Pause.*] The
day is now well advanced. [*Smile.*] To speak in the old
style. [*Smile off.*] And yet it is perhaps a little soon for
my song. [*Pause.*] To sing too soon is a great mistake, I
find. [*Turning towards bag.*] There is of course the bag.
[*Looking at bag.*] The bag. [*Back front.*] Could I
enumerate its contents? [*Pause.*] No. [*Pause.*] Could I, if
some kind person were to come along and ask, What
all have you got in that big black bag, Winnie? give an
exhaustive answer? [*Pause.*] No. [*Pause.*] The depths in
particular, who knows what treasures. [*Pause.*] What
comforts. [*Turns to look at bag.*] Yes, there is the bag.
[*Back front.*] But something tells me, Do not overdo the
bag, Winnie, make use of it of course, let it help
you . . . along, when stuck, by all means, but cast your
mind forward, something tells me, cast your mind
forward, Winnie, to the time when words must fail—

[*she closes eyes, pause, opens eyes*]—and do not overdo
the bag. [*Pause. She turns to look at bag.*] Perhaps just
one quick dip. [*She turns back front, closes eyes, throws out
left arm, plunges hand in bag and brings out revolver.
Disgusted.*] You again! [*She opens eyes, brings revolver front
and contemplates it. She weighs it in her palm.*] You'd
think the weight of this thing would bring it down
among the . . . last rounds. But no. It doesn't. Ever
uppermost, like Browning. [*Pause.*] Brownie . . .
[*Turning a little towards Willie.*] Remember Brownie,
Willie? [*Pause.*] Remember how you used to keep on at
me to take it away from you? Take it away, Winnie,
take it away, before I put myself out of my misery.
[*Back front. Derisive.*] *Your* misery! [*To revolver.*] Oh I
suppose it's a comfort to know you're there, but I'm
tired of you. [*Pause.*] I'll leave you out, that's what I'll
do. [*She lays revolver on ground to her right.*] There, that's
your home from this day out. [*Smile.*] The old style!
[*Smile off.*] And now? [*Long pause.*] Is gravity what it
was, Willie, I fancy not. [*Pause.*] Yes, the feeling more
and more that if I were not held—[*gesture*]—in this
way, I would simply float up into the blue. [*Pause.*] And
that perhaps some day the earth will yield and let me

go, the pull is so great, yes, crack all round me and let me out. [*Pause.*] Don't you ever have that feeling, Willie, of being sucked up? [*Pause.*] Don't you have to cling on sometimes, Willie? [*Pause. She turns a little towards him.*] Willie. [*Pause.*]

WILLIE   *Sucked* up?

WINNIE   Yes love, up into the blue, like gossamer. [*Pause.*] No? [*Pause.*] You don't? [*Pause.*] Ah well, natural laws, natural laws, I suppose it's like everything else, it all depends on the creature you happen to be. All I can say is for my part is that for me they are not what they were when I was young and . . . foolish and . . . [*faltering, head down*] . . . beautiful . . . possibly . . . lovely . . . in a way . . . to look at. [*Pause. Head up.*] Forgive me, Willie, sorrow keeps breaking in. [*Normal voice.*] Ah well what a joy in any case to know you are there, as usual, and perhaps awake, and perhaps taking all this in, some of all this, what a happy day for me . . . it will have been. [*Pause.*] So far. [*Pause.*] What a blessing nothing grows, imagine if all this stuff were to start growing. [*Pause.*] Imagine. [*Pause.*]

Ah yes, great mercies. [*Long pause.*] I can say no more. [*Pause.*] For the moment. [*Pause. Turns to look at bag. Back front. Smile.*] No no. [*Smile off. Looks at parasol.*] I suppose I might—[*takes up parasol*]—yes, I suppose I might . . . hoist this thing now. [*Begins to unfurl it. Following punctuated by mechanical difficulties overcome.*] One keeps putting off—putting up—for fear of putting up—too soon—and the day goes by—quite by—without one's having put up—at all. [*Parasol now fully open. Turned to her right she twirls it idly this way and that.*] Ah yes, so little to say, so little to do, and the fear so great, certain days, of finding oneself . . . left, with hours still to run, before the bell for sleep, and nothing more to say, nothing more to do, that the days go by, certain days go by, quite by, the bell goes, and little or nothing said, little or nothing done. [*Raising parasol.*] That is the danger. [*Turning front.*] To be guarded against. [*She gazes front, holding up parasol with right hand. Maximum pause.*] I used to perspire freely. [*Pause.*] Now hardly at all. [*Pause.*] The heat is much greater. [*Pause.*] The perspiration much less. [*Pause.*] That is what I find so wonderful. [*Pause.*] The way man adapts himself. [*Pause.*] To changing conditions. [*She transfers parasol to left hand. Long pause.*] Holding up wearies the arm. [*Pause.*] Not if one is going along. [*Pause.*] Only if one is at rest. [*Pause.*] That is a curious observation. [*Pause.*] I hope you heard that, Willie, I should be grieved to think you had not heard that. [*She takes parasol in both hands. Long pause.*] I am weary, holding it up, and I cannot put it down. [*Pause.*] I am worse off with it up than with it down, and I cannot put it down. [*Pause.*] Reason says, Put it down, Winnie, it is not helping you, put the thing down and get on with something else. [*Pause.*] I cannot. [*Pause.*] I cannot move. [*Pause.*] No, something must happen, in the world, take place, some change, I cannot, if I am to move again. [*Pause.*] Willie. [*Mildly.*] Help. [*Pause.*] No? [*Pause.*] Bid me put this thing down, Willie, I would obey you instantly, as I have always done, honoured and obeyed. [*Pause.*] Please, Willie. [*Mildly.*] For pity's sake. [*Pause.*] No? [*Pause.*] You can't? [*Pause.*] Well I don't blame you, no, it would ill become me, who cannot move, to blame my Willie because he cannot speak. [*Pause.*] Fortunately I am in tongue again. [*Pause.*] That is what I find so wonderful, my two lamps, when one goes out the other burns brighter. [*Pause.*] Oh yes, great mercies. [*Maximum pause. The parasol goes on fire. Smoke, flames if feasible. She sniffs, looks up, throws parasol to her right behind mound, cranes back to watch it burning. Pause.*] Ah earth you old extinguisher. [*Back front.*] I presume this has occurred before, though I cannot recall it. [*Pause.*] Can you, Willie? [*Turns a little towards him.*] Can you recall this having occurred before? [*Pause. Cranes back to look at him.*] Do you know what has occurred, Willie? [*Pause.*] Have you gone off on me again? [*Pause.*] I do not ask if you are alive to all that is going on, I merely ask if you have not gone off on me again. [*Pause.*] Your eyes appear to be closed, but that has no particular significance we know. [*Pause.*] Raise a finger, dear, will you please, if you are not quite senseless. [*Pause.*] Do that for me, Willie please, just the little finger, if you are still conscious. [*Pause. Joyful.*] Oh all five, you are a darling today, now I may continue with an easy mind. [*Back front.*] Yes, what ever occurred that did not occur before and yet . . . I wonder, yes, I confess I wonder. [*Pause.*] With the sun blazing so much fiercer down, and hourly fiercer, is it not natural things should go on fire never known to do so, in this way I mean,

spontaneous like. [*Pause.*] Shall I myself not melt
perhaps in the end, or burn, oh I do not mean
necessarily burst into flames, no, just little by little be
charred to a black cinder, all this—[*ample gesture of
arms*]—visible flesh. [*Pause.*] On the other hand, did I
ever know a temperate time? [*Pause.*] No. [*Pause.*] I
speak of temperate times and torrid times, they are
empty words. [*Pause.*] I speak of when I was not yet
caught—in this way—and had my legs and had the
use of my legs, and could seek out a shady place, like
you, when I was tired of the sun, or a sunny place
when I was tired of the shade, like you, and they are
all empty words. [*Pause.*] It is no hotter today than
yesterday, it will be no hotter tomorrow than today,
how could it, and so on back into the far past, forward
into the far future. [*Pause.*] And should one day the
earth cover my breasts, then I shall never have seen
my breasts, no one ever seen my breasts. [*Pause.*] I
hope you caught something of that, Willie, I should
be sorry to think you had caught nothing of all that, it
is not every day I rise to such heights. [*Pause.*] Yes,
something seems to have occurred, something has
seemed to occur, and nothing has occurred, nothing

at all, you are quite right, Willie. [*Pause.*] The sunshade
will be there again tomorrow, beside me on this
mound, to help me through the day. [*Pause. She takes
up mirror.*] I take up this little glass, I shiver it on a
stone—[*does so*]—I throw it away—[*does so far behind
her*]—it will be in the bag again tomorrow, without a
scratch, to help me through the day. [*Pause.*] No, one
can do nothing. [*Pause.*] That is what I find so
wonderful, the way things . . . [*voice breaks, head
down*] . . . things . . . so wonderful. [*Long pause, head
down. Finally turns, still bowed, to bag, brings out
unidentifiable odds and ends, stuffs them back, fumbles
deeper, brings out finally musical-box, winds it up, turns it
on, listens for a moment holding it in both hands, huddled
over it, turns back front, straightens up and listens to tune,
holding box to breast with both hands. It plays the Waltz
Duet "I love you so" from* The Merry Widow. *Gradually
happy expression. She sways to the rhythm. Music stops.
Pause. Brief burst of hoarse song without words—musical-
box tune—from Willie. Increase of happy expression. She
lays down box.*] Oh this will have been a happy day! [*She
claps hands.*] Again, Willie, again! [*Claps.*] Encore, Willie,
please! [*Pause. Happy expression off.*] No? You won't do

that for me? [*Pause.*] Well it is very understandable,
very understandable. One cannot sing just to please
someone, however much one loves them, no, song
must come from the heart, that is what I always say,
pour out from the inmost, like a thrush. [*Pause.*] How
often I have said, in evil hours, Sing now, Winnie, sing
your song, there is nothing else for it, and did not.
[*Pause.*] Could not. [*Pause.*] No, like the thrush, or the
bird of dawning, with no thought of benefit, to
oneself or anyone else. [*Pause.*] And now? [*Long pause.
Low.*] Strange feeling. [*Pause. Do.*] Strange feeling that
someone is looking at me. I am clear, then dim, then
gone, then dim again, then clear again, and so on,
back and forth, in and out of someone's eye. [*Pause.
Do.*] Strange? [*Pause. Do.*] No, here all is strange. [*Pause.
Normal voice.*] Something says, Stop talking now,
Winnie, for a minute, don't squander all your words
for the day, stop talking and do something for a
change, will you? [*She raises hands and holds them open
before her eyes. Apostrophic.*] Do something! [*She closes
hands.*] What claws! [*She turns to bag, rummages in it,
brings out finally a nailfile, turns back front and begins to
file nails. Files for a time in silence, then the following*

punctuated by filing.] There floats up—into my thoughts—a Mr. Shower—a Mr. and perhaps a Mrs. Shower—no—they are holding hands—his fiancée then more likely—or just some—loved one. [*Looks closer at nails.*] Very brittle today. [*Resumes filing.*] Shower—Shower—does the name mean anything— to you, Willie—evoke any reality, I mean—for you, Willie—don't answer if you don't—feel up to it—you have done more—than your bit—already—Shower— Shower. [*Inspects filed nails.*] Bit more like it. [*Raises head, gazes front.*] Keep yourself nice, Winnie, that's what I always say, come what may, keep yourself nice. [*Pause. Resumes filing.*] Yes—Shower—Shower—[*stops filing, raises head, gazes front, pause*]—or Cooker, perhaps I should say Cooker. [*Turning a little towards Willie.*] Cooker, Willie, does Cooker strike a chord? [*Pause. Turns a little further. Louder.*] Cooker, Willie, does Cooker ring a bell, the name Cooker? [*Pause. She cranes back to look at him. Pause.*] Oh really! [*Pause.*] Have you no handkerchief, darling? [*Pause.*] Have you no delicacy? [*Pause.*] Oh, Willie, you're not eating it! Spit it out, dear, spit it out! [*Pause. Back front.*] Ah well, I suppose it's only natural. [*Break in voice.*] Human.

[*Pause. Do.*] What *is* one to do? [*Head down. Do.*] All day
long. [*Pause. Do.*] Day after day. [*Pause. Head up. Smile.
Calm.*] The old style! [*Smile off. Resumes nails.*] No, done
him. [*Passes on to next.*] Should have put on my glasses.
[*Pause.*] Too late now. [*Finishes left hand, inspects it.*] Bit
more human. [*Starts right hand. Following punctuated as
before.*] Well anyway—this man Shower—or Cooker—
no matter—and the woman—hand in hand—in the
other hands bags—kind of big brown grips—
standing there gaping at me—and at last this man
Shower—or Cooker—ends in er anyway—stake my
life on that—What's she doing? he says—What's the
idea? he says—stuck up to her diddies in the bleeding
ground—coarse fellow—What does it mean? he
says—What's it meant to mean?—and so on—lot
more stuff like that—usual drivel—Do you hear me?
he says—I do, she says, God help me—What do you
mean, he says, God help you? [*Stops filing, raises head,
gazes front.*] And you, she says, what's the idea of you,
she says, what are you meant to mean? It is because
you're still on your two flat feet, with your old ditty
full of tinned muck and changes of underwear,
dragging me up and down this fornicating wilderness,

coarse creature, fit mate—[*with sudden violence*]—let
go of my hand and drop for God's sake, she says, drop!
[*Pause. Resumes filing.*] Why doesn't he dig her out? he
says—referring to you, my dear—What good is she to
him like that?—What good is he to her like that?—
and so on—usual tosh—Good! she says, have a heart
for God's sake—Dig her out, he says, dig her out, no
sense in her like that—Dig her out with what? she
says—I'd dig her out with my bare hands, he says—
must have been man and—wife. [*Files in silence.*] Next
thing they're away—hand in hand—and the bags—
dim—then gone—last human kind—to stray this
way. [*Finishes right hand, inspects it, lays down file, gazes
front.*] Strange thing, time like this, drift up into the
mind. [*Pause.*] Strange? [*Pause.*] No, here all is strange.
[*Pause.*] Thankful for it in any case. [*Voice breaks.*] Most
thankful. [*Head down. Pause. Head up. Calm.*] Bow and
raise the head, bow and raise, always that. [*Pause.*] And
now? [*Long pause. Starts putting things back in bag,
toothbrush last. This operation, interrupted by pauses as
indicated, punctuates following.*] It is perhaps a little
soon—to make ready—for the night—[*stops tidying,
head up, smile*]—the old style!—[*smile off, resumes

tidying]—and yet I do—make ready for the night—
feeling it at hand—the bell for sleep—saying to
myself—Winnie—it will not be long now, Winnie—
until the bell for sleep. [*Stops tidying, head up.*]
Sometimes I am wrong. [*Smile.*] But not often. [*Smile
off.*] Sometimes all is over, for the day, all done, all
said, all ready for the night, and the day not over, far
from over, the night not ready, far, far from ready.
[*Smile.*] But not often. [*Smile off.*] Yes, the bell for sleep,
when I feel it at hand, and so make ready for the
night—[*gesture*]—in this way, sometimes I am
wrong—[*smile*]—but not often. [*Smile off. Resumes
tidying.*] I used to think—I say I used to think—that
all these things—put back into the bag—if too
soon—put back too soon—could be taken out
again—if necessary—if needed—and so on—
indefinitely—back into the bag—back out of the
bag—until the bell—went. [*Stops tidying, head up,
smile.*] But no. [*Smile broader.*] No no. [*Smile off. Resumes
tidying.*] I suppose this—might seem strange—this—
what shall I say—this what I have said—yes—[*she
takes up revolver*]—strange—[*she turns to put revolver in
bag*]—were it not—[*about to put revolver in bag she*

arrests gesture and turns back front]—were it not—[*she lays down revolver to her right, stops tidying, head up*]— that all seems strange. [*Pause.*] Most strange. [*Pause.*] Never any change. [*Pause.*] And more and more strange. [*Pause. She bends to mound again, takes up last object, i.e. toothbrush, and turns to put it in bag when her attention is drawn to disturbance from Willie. She cranes back and to her right to see. Pause.*] Weary of your hole, dear? [*Pause.*] Well I can understand that. [*Pause.*] Don't forget your straw. [*Pause.*] Not the crawler you were, poor darling. [*Pause.*] No, not the crawler I gave my heart to. [*Pause.*] The hands and knees, love, try the hands and knees. [*Pause.*] The knees! The knees! [*Pause.*] What a curse, mobility! [*She follows with eyes his progress towards her behind mound, i.e. towards place he occupied at beginning of act.*] Another foot, Willie, and you're home. [*Pause as she observes last foot.*] Ah! [*Turns back front laboriously, rubs neck.*] Crick in my neck admiring you. [*Rubs neck.*] But it's worth it, well worth it. [*Turning slightly towards him.*] Do you know what I dream sometimes? [*Pause.*] What I dream sometimes, Willie. [*Pause.*] That you'll come round and live this side where I could see you. [*Pause. Back front.*] I'd be a different woman. [*Pause.*] Unrecognizable. [*Turning slightly towards him.*] Or just now and then, come round this side just every now and then and let me feast on you. [*Back front.*] But you can't, I know. [*Head down.*] I know. [*Pause. Head up.*] Well anyway— [*looks at toothbrush in her hand*]—can't be long now [*looks at brush*]—until the bell. [*Top back of Willie's head appears above slope. Winnie looks closer at brush.*] Fully guaranteed ... [*head up*] ... what's this it was? [*Willie's hand appears with handkerchief, spreads it on skull, disappears.*] Genuine pure ... fully guaranteed ... [*Willie's hand appears with boater, settles it on head, rakish angle, disappears*] ... genuine pure ... ah! hog's setae. [*Pause.*] What is a hog exactly? [*Pause. Turns slightly towards Willie.*] What exactly is a hog, Willie, do you know, I can't remember. [*Pause. Turning a little further, pleading.*] What *is* a hog, Willie, please! [*Pause.*]

WILLIE   Castrated male swine. [*Happy expression appears on Winnie's face.*] Reared for slaughter.

[*Happy expression increases. Willie opens newspaper, hands invisible. Tops of yellow sheets appear on either side of his head. Winnie gazes before her with happy expression.*]

WINNIE Oh this *is* a happy day! This will have been another happy day! [*Pause.*] After all. [*Pause.*] So far.

[*Pause. Happy expression off. Willie turns page. Pause. He turns another page. Pause.*]

WILLIE Opening for smart youth.

[*Pause. Winnie takes off hat, turns to put it in bag, arrests gesture, turns back front. Smile.*]

WINNIE No. [*Smile broader.*] No no. [*Smile off. Puts on hat again, gazes front, pause.*] And now? [*Pause.*] Sing. [*Pause.*] Sing your song, Winnie. [*Pause.*] No? [*Pause.*] Then pray. [*Pause.*] Pray your prayer, Winnie.

[*Pause. Willie turns page. Pause.*]

WILLIE Wanted bright boy.

[*Pause. Winnie gazes before her. Willie turns page. Pause. Newspaper disappears. Long pause.*]

WINNIE   Pray your old prayer, Winnie.

[*Long pause.*]

Curtain

ACT II

Scene as before.

Winnie imbedded up to neck, hat on head, eyes closed. Her head, which she can no longer turn, nor bow, nor raise, faces front motionless throughout act. Movements of eyes as indicated.

Bag and parasol as before. Revolver conspicuous to her right on mound.

Long pause.

Bell rings loudly. She opens eyes at once. Bell stops. She gazes front. Long pause.

WINNIE Hail, holy light. [*Long pause. She closes her eyes. Bell rings loudly. She opens eyes at once. Bell stops. She gazes front. Long smile. Smile off. Long pause.*] Someone is looking at me still. [*Pause.*] Caring for me still. [*Pause.*] That is what I find so wonderful. [*Pause.*] Eyes on my eyes. [*Pause.*] What is that unforgettable line? [*Pause. Eyes right.*] Willie. [*Pause. Louder.*] Willie. [*Pause. Eyes front.*] May one still speak of time? [*Pause.*] Say it is a long time now, Willie, since I saw you. [*Pause.*] Since I heard you. [*Pause.*] May one? [*Pause.*] One does. [*Smile.*] The old style! [*Smile off.*] There is so little one can speak of.

[*Pause.*] One speaks of it all. [*Pause.*] All one can. [*Pause.*] I used to think ... [*pause*] ... I say I used to think that I would learn to talk alone. [*Pause.*] By that I mean to myself, the wilderness. [*Smile.*] But no. [*Smile broader.*] No no. [*Smile off.*] Ergo you are there. [*Pause.*] Oh no doubt you are dead, like the others, no doubt you have died, or gone away and left me, like the others, it doesn't matter, you are there. [*Pause. Eyes left.*] The bag too is there, the same as ever, I can see it. [*Pause. Eyes right. Louder.*] The bag is there, Willie, as good as ever, the one you gave me that day ... to go to market. [*Pause. Eyes front.*] That day. [*Pause.*] What day? [*Pause.*] I used to pray. [*Pause.*] I say I used to pray. [*Pause.*] Yes, I must confess I did. [*Smile.*] Not now. [*Smile broader.*] No no. [*Smile off. Pause.*] Then ... now ... what difficulties here, for the mind. [*Pause.*] To have been always what I am—and so changed from what I was. [*Pause.*] I am the one, I say the one, then the other. [*Pause.*] Now the one, then the other. [*Pause.*] There is so little one can say, one says it all. [*Pause.*] All one can. [*Pause.*] And no truth in it anywhere. [*Pause.*] My arms. [*Pause.*] My breasts. [*Pause.*] What arms? [*Pause.*] What breasts? [*Pause.*] Willie. [*Pause.*] What Willie? [*Sudden *vehement affirmation.*] My Willie! [*Eyes right, calling.*]

Willie! [*Pause. Louder.*] Willie! [*Pause. Eyes front.*] Ah

well, not to know, not to know for sure, great mercy,

all I ask. [*Pause.*] Ah yes . . . then . . . now . . . beechen

green . . . this . . . Charlie . . . kisses . . . this . . . all

that . . . deep trouble for the mind. [*Pause.*] But it does

not trouble mine. [*Smile.*] Not now. [*Smile broader.*] No

no. [*Smile off. Long pause. She closes eyes. Bell rings loudly.

She opens eyes. Pause.*] Eyes float up that seem to close

in peace . . . to see . . . in peace. [*Pause.*] Not mine.

[*Smile.*] Not now. [*Smile broader.*] No no. [*Smile off. Long

pause.*] Willie. [*Pause.*] Do you think the earth has lost

its atmosphere, Willie? [*Pause.*] Do you, Willie? [*Pause.*]

You have no opinion? [*Pause.*] Well that is like you, you

never had any opinion about anything. [*Pause.*] It's

understandable. [*Pause.*] Most. [*Pause.*] The earthball.

[*Pause.*] I sometimes wonder. [*Pause.*] Perhaps not

quite all. [*Pause.*] There always remains something.

[*Pause.*] Of everything. [*Pause.*] Some remains. [*Pause.*]

If the mind were to go. [*Pause.*] It won't of course.

[*Pause.*] Not quite. [*Pause.*] Not mine. [*Smile.*] Not now.

[*Smile broader.*] No no. [*Smile off. Long pause.*] It might

be the eternal cold. [*Pause.*] Everlasting perishing cold.

[*Pause.*] Just chance, I take it, happy chance. [*Pause.*] Oh yes, great mercies, great mercies. [*Pause.*] And now? [*Long pause.*] The face. [*Pause.*] The nose. [*She squints down.*] I can see it . . . [*squinting down*] . . . the tip . . . the nostrils . . . breath of life . . . that curve you so admired [*pouts*] . . . a hint of lip . . . [*pouts again*] . . . if I pout them out . . . [*sticks out tongue*] . . . the tongue of course . . . you so admired . . . if I stick it out . . . [*sticks it out again*] . . . the tip . . . [*eyes up*] . . . suspicion of brow . . . eyebrow . . . imagination possibly . . . [*eyes left*] . . . cheek . . . no . . . [*eyes right*] . . . no . . . [*distends cheeks*] . . . even if I puff them out . . . [*eyes left, distends cheeks again*] . . . no . . . no damask. [*Eyes front.*] That is all. [*Pause.*] The bag of course . . . [*eyes left*] . . . a little blurred perhaps . . . but the bag. [*Eyes front. Offhand.*] The earth of course and sky. [*Eyes right.*] The sunshade you gave me . . . that day . . . [*pause*] . . . that day . . . the lake . . . the reeds. [*Eyes front. Pause.*] What day? [*Pause.*] What reeds? [*Long pause. Eyes close. Bell rings loudly. Eyes open. Pause. Eyes right.*] Brownie of course. [*Pause.*] You remember Brownie, Willie, I can see him. [*Pause.*] Brownie is there, Willie, beside me. [*Pause. Loud.*] Brownie is there, Willie. [*Pause. Eyes front.*] That is all.

[*Pause.*] What would I do without them? [*Pause.*] What would I do without them, when words fail? [*Pause.*] Gaze before me, with compressed lips. [*Long pause while she does so.*] I cannot. [*Pause.*] Ah yes, great mercies, great mercies. [*Long pause. Low.*] Sometimes I hear sounds. [*Listening expression. Normal voice.*] But not often. [*Pause.*] They are a boon, sounds are a boon, they help me . . . through the day. [*Smile.*] The old style! [*Smile off.*] Yes, those are happy days, when there are sounds. [*Pause.*] When I hear sounds. [*Pause.*] I used to think . . . [*pause*] . . . I say I used to think they were in my head. [*Smile.*] But no. [*Smile broader.*] No no. [*Smile off.*] That was just logic. [*Pause.*] Reason. [*Pause.*] I have not lost my reason. [*Pause.*] Not yet. [*Pause.*] Not all. [*Pause.*] Some remains. [*Pause.*] Sounds. [*Pause.*] Like little . . . sunderings, little falls . . . apart. [*Pause. Low.*] It's things, Willie. [*Pause. Normal voice.*] In the bag, outside the bag. [*Pause.*] Ah yes, things have their life, that is what I always say, *things* have a life. [*Pause.*] Take my looking-glass, it doesn't need me. [*Pause.*] The bell. [*Pause.*] It hurts like a knife. [*Pause.*] A gouge. [*Pause.*] One cannot ignore it. [*Pause.*] How often . . . [*pause*] . . . I say how often I have said, Ignore it,

Winnie, ignore the bell, pay no heed, just sleep and wake, sleep and wake, as you please, open and close the eyes, as you please, or in the way you find most helpful. [*Pause.*] Open and close the eyes, Winnie, open and close, always that. [*Pause.*] But no. [*Smile.*] Not now. [*Smile broader.*] No no. [*Smile off. Pause.*] What now? [*Pause.*] What now, Willie? [*Long pause.*] There is my story of course, when all else fails. [*Pause.*] A life. [*Smile.*] A long life. [*Smile off.*] Beginning in the womb, where life used to begin, Mildred has memories, she will have memories, of the womb, before she dies, the mother's womb. [*Pause.*] She is now four or five already and has recently been given a big waxen dolly. [*Pause.*] Fully clothed, complete outfit. [*Pause.*] Shoes, socks, undies, complete set, frilly frock, gloves. [*Pause.*] White mesh. [*Pause.*] A little white straw hat with a chin elastic. [*Pause.*] Pearly necklet. [*Pause.*] A little picture-book with legends in real print to go under her arm when she takes her walk. [*Pause.*] China blue eyes that open and shut. [*Pause. Narrative.*] The sun was not well up when Milly rose, descended the steep . . . [*pause*] . . . slipped on her nightgown, descended all alone the steep wooden stairs, backwards on all fours, though she had been forbidden to do so, entered the ... [*pause*] ... tiptoed down the silent passage, entered the nursery and began to undress Dolly. [*Pause.*] Crept under the table and began to undress Dolly. [*Pause.*] Scolding her ... the while. [*Pause.*] Suddenly a mouse— [*Long pause.*] Gently, Winnie. [*Long pause. Calling.*] Willie! [*Pause. Louder.*] Willie! [*Pause. Mild reproach.*] I sometimes find your attitude a little strange, Willie, all this time, it is not like you to be wantonly cruel. [*Pause.*] Strange? [*Pause.*] No. [*Smile.*] Not here. [*Smile broader.*] Not now. [*Smile off.*] And yet ... [*Suddenly anxious.*] I do hope nothing is amiss. [*Eyes right, loud.*] Is all well, dear? [*Pause. Eyes front. To herself.*] God grant he did not go in head foremost! [*Eyes right, loud.*] You're not stuck, Willie? [*Pause. Do.*] You're not jammed, Willie? [*Eyes front, distressed.*] Perhaps he is crying out for help all this time and I do not hear him! [*Pause.*] I do of course hear cries. [*Pause.*] But they are in my head surely. [*Pause.*] Is it possible that ... [*Pause. With finality.*] No no, my head was always full of cries. [*Pause.*] Faint confused cries. [*Pause.*] They come. [*Pause.*] Then go. [*Pause.*] As on a wind. [*Pause.*] That is what I find so

wonderful. [*Pause.*] They cease. [*Pause.*] Ah yes, great
mercies, great mercies. [*Pause.*] The day is now well
advanced. [*Smile. Smile off.*] And yet it is perhaps a little
soon for my song. [*Pause.*] To sing too soon is fatal, I
always find. [*Pause.*] On the other hand it is possible to
leave it too late. [*Pause.*] The bell goes for sleep and
one has not sung. [*Pause.*] The whole day has flown—
[*smile, smile off*]—flown by, quite by, and no song of
any class, kind or description. [*Pause.*] There is a
problem here. [*Pause.*] One cannot sing . . . just like
that, no. [*Pause.*] It bubbles up, for some unknown
reason, the time is ill chosen, one chokes it back.
[*Pause.*] One says, Now is the time, it is now or never,
and one cannot. [*Pause.*] Simply cannot sing. [*Pause.*]
Not a note. [*Pause.*] Another thing, Willie, while we are
on this subject. [*Pause.*] The sadness after song. [*Pause.*]
Have you run across that, Willie? [*Pause.*] In the course
of your experience. [*Pause.*] No? [*Pause.*] Sadness after
intimate sexual intercourse one is familiar with of
course. [*Pause.*] You would concur with Aristotle there,
Willie, I fancy. [*Pause.*] Yes, that one knows and is
prepared to face. [*Pause.*] But after song . . . [*Pause.*] It
does not last of course. [*Pause.*] That is what I find so

wonderful. [*Pause.*] It wears away. [*Pause.*] What are
those exquisite lines? [*Pause.*] Go forget me why
should something o'er that something shadow
fling . . . go forget me . . . why should sorrow . . .
brightly smile . . . go forget me . . . never hear me . . .
sweetly smile . . . brightly sing . . . [*Pause. With a sigh.*]
One loses one's classics. [*Pause.*] Oh not all. [*Pause.*]
A part. [*Pause.*] A part remains. [*Pause.*] That is what I
find so wonderful, a part remains, of one's classics, to
help one through the day. [*Pause.*] Oh yes, many
mercies, many mercies. [*Pause.*] And now? [*Pause.*]
And now, Willie? [*Long pause.*] I call to the eye of the
mind . . . Mr. Shower—or Cooker. [*She closes her eyes.
Bell rings loudly. She opens her eyes. Pause.*] Hand in
hand, in the other hands bags. [*Pause.*] Getting on . . .
in life. [*Pause.*] No longer young, not yet old. [*Pause.*]
Standing there gaping at me. [*Pause.*] Can't have been a
bad bosom, he says, in its day. [*Pause.*] Seen worse
shoulders, he says, in my time. [*Pause.*] Does she feel
her legs? he says. [*Pause.*] Is there any life in her legs?
he says [*Pause.*] Has she anything on underneath? he
says. [*Pause.*] Ask her, he says, I'm shy. [*Pause.*] Ask her
what? she says. [*Pause.*] Is there any life in her legs.

[*Pause.*] Has she anything on underneath. [*Pause.*] Ask her yourself, she says. [*Pause. With sudden violence.*] Let go of me for Christ sake and drop! [*Pause. Do.*] Drop dead! [*Smile.*] But no. [*Smile broader.*] No no. [*Smile off.*] I watch them recede. [*Pause.*] Hand in hand—and the bags. [*Pause.*] Dim. [*Pause.*] Then gone. [*Pause.*] Last human kind—to stray this way. [*Pause.*] Up to date. [*Pause.*] And now? [*Pause. Low.*] Help. [*Pause. Do.*] Help, Willie. [*Pause. Do.*] No? [*Long pause. Narrative.*] Suddenly a mouse . . . [*Pause.*] Suddenly a mouse ran up her little thigh and Mildred, dropping Dolly in her fright, began to scream—[*Winnie gives a sudden piercing scream*]—and screamed and screamed—[*Winnie screams twice*]—screamed and screamed and screamed and screamed till all came running, in their night attire, papa, mamma, Bibby and . . . old Annie, to see what was the matter . . . [*pause*] . . . what on earth could possibly be the matter. [*Pause.*] Too late. [*Pause.*] Too late. [*Long pause. Just audible.*] Willie. [*Pause. Normal voice.*] Ah well, not long now, Winnie, can't be long now, until the bell for sleep. [*Pause.*] Then you may close your eyes, then you *must* close your eyes— and keep them closed. [*Pause.*] Why say that again?

[*Pause.*] I used to think ... [*pause*] ... I say I used to think there was no difference between one fraction of a second and the next. [*Pause.*] I used to say ... [*pause*] ... I say I used to say, Winnie, you are changeless, there is never any difference between one fraction of a second and the next. [*Pause.*] Why bring that up again? [*Pause.*] There is so little one can bring up, one brings up all. [*Pause.*] All one can. [*Pause.*] My neck is hurting me. [*Pause. With sudden violence.*] My neck is hurting me! [*Pause.*] Ah that's better. [*With mild irritation.*] Everything within reason. [*Long pause.*] I can do no more. [*Pause.*] Say no more. [*Pause.*] But I must say more. [*Pause.*] Problem here. [*Pause.*] No, something must move, in the world, I can't any more. [*Pause.*] A zephyr. [*Pause.*] A breath. [*Pause.*] What are those immortal lines? [*Pause.*] It might be the eternal dark. [*Pause.*] Black night without end. [*Pause.*] Just chance, I take it, happy chance. [*Pause.*] Oh yes, abounding mercies. [*Long pause.*] And now? [*Pause.*] And now, Willie? [*Long pause.*] That day. [*Pause.*] The pink fizz. [*Pause.*] The flute glasses. [*Pause.*] The last guest gone. [*Pause.*] The last bumper with the bodies nearly touching. [*Pause.*] The look. [*Long pause.*]

What day? [*Long pause.*] What look? [*Long pause.*] I hear
cries. [*Pause.*] Sing. [*Pause.*] Sing your old song, Winnie.
[*Long pause. Suddenly alert expression. Eyes switch right.
Willie's head appears to her right round corner of mound.
He is on all fours, dressed to kill—top hat, morning coat,
striped trousers, etc., white gloves in hand. Very long bushy
white Battle of Britain moustache. He halts, gazes front,
smooths moustache. He emerges completely from behind
mound, turns to his left, halts, looks up at Winnie. He
advances on all fours towards centre, halts, turns head front,
gazes front, strokes moustache, straightens tie, adjusts hat,
advances a little further, halts, takes off hat and looks up at
Winnie. He is now not far from centre and within her field
of vision. Unable to sustain effort of looking up he sinks
head to ground.*]

WINNIE   [*mondaine*] Well this is an unexpected pleasure! [*Pause.*]
Reminds me of the day you came whining for my
hand. [*Pause.*] I worship you, Winnie, be mine.
[*He looks up.*] Life a mockery without Win. [*She goes
off into a giggle.*] What a get up, you do look a sight!
[*Giggles.*] Where are the flowers? [*Pause.*] That smile
today. [*Willie sinks head.*] What's that on your neck, an

anthrax? [*Pause.*] Want to watch that, Willie, before it
gets a hold on you. [*Pause.*] Where were you all this
time? [*Pause.*] What were you doing all this time?
[*Pause.*] Changing? [*Pause.*] Did you not hear me
screaming for you? [*Pause.*] Did you get stuck in your
hole? [*Pause. He looks up.*] That's right, Willie, look at
me. [*Pause.*] Feast your old eyes, Willie. [*Pause.*] Does
anything remain? [*Pause.*] Any remains? [*Pause.*] No?
[*Pause.*] I haven't been able to look after it, you know.
[*He sinks his head.*] You are still recognizable, in a way.
[*Pause.*] Are you thinking of coming to live this side
now . . . for a bit maybe? [*Pause.*] No? [*Pause.*] Just a
brief call? [*Pause.*] Have you gone deaf, Willie? [*Pause.*]
Dumb? [*Pause.*] Oh I know you were never one to talk,
I worship you Winnie be mine and then nothing from
that day forth only titbits from Reynolds' News. [*Eyes
front. Pause.*] Ah well, what matter, that's what I always
say, it will have been a happy day, after all, another
happy day. [*Pause.*] Not long now, Winnie. [*Pause.*]
I hear cries. [*Pause.*] Do you ever hear cries, Willie?
[*Pause.*] No? [*Eyes back on Willie.*] Willie. [*Pause.*] Look at
me again, Willie. [*Pause.*] Once more, Willie. [*He looks
up. Happily.*] Ah! [*Pause. Shocked.*] What ails you, Willie,

I never saw such an expression! [*Pause.*] Put on your hat, dear, it's the sun, don't stand on ceremony, I won't mind. [*He drops hat and gloves and starts to crawl up mound towards her. Gleeful.*] Oh I say, this is terrific! [*He halts, clinging to mound with one hand, reaching up with the other.*] Come on, dear, put a bit of jizz into it, I'll cheer you on. [*Pause.*] Is it me you're after, Willie . . . or is it something else? [*Pause.*] Do you want to touch my face . . . again? [*Pause.*] Is it a kiss you're after, Willie . . . or is it something else? [*Pause.*] There was a time when I could have given you a hand. [*Pause.*] And then a time before that again when I did give you a hand. [*Pause.*] You were always in dire need of a hand, Willie. [*He slithers back to foot of mound and lies with face to ground.*] Brrum! [*Pause. He rises to hands and knees, raises his face towards her.*] Have another go, Willie, I'll cheer you on. [*Pause.*] Don't look at me like that! [*Pause. Vehement.*] Don't look at me like that! [*Pause. Low.*] Have you gone off your head, Willie? [*Pause. Do.*] Out of your poor old wits, Willie?

[*Pause.*]

WILLIE   [*just audible*] Win.

[*Pause. Winnie's eyes front. Happy expression appears, grows.*]

WINNIE   Win! [*Pause.*] Oh this *is* a happy day, this will have been another happy day! [*Pause.*] After all. [*Pause.*] So far.

[*Pause. She hums tentatively beginning of song, then sings softly, musical-box tune.*]

> Though I say not
> What I may not
> Let you hear,
> Yet the swaying
> Dance is saying,
> Love me dear!
> Every touch of fingers
> Tells me what I know,
> Says for you,
> It's true, it's true,
> You love me so!

[*Pause. Happy expression off. She closes her eyes. Bell rings loudly. She opens her eyes. She smiles, gazing front. She turns her eyes, smiling, to Willie, still on his hands and knees looking up at her. Smile off. They look at each other. Long pause.*]

Curtain